If You Give an Ox an Oxy

A Parad(ox)y

Dr. Laura E. Happe, PharmD, MPH

Illustrations by Bryan Nigh

T0098603

NEW YORK

LONDON • NASHVILLE • MELBOURNE • VANCOUVER

If You Give an Ox an Oxy - A Parad(ox)y

Published in New York, New York, by Morgan James Publishing. Morgan James is a trademark of Morgan James, LLC. www.MorganJamesPublishing.com

ISBN 9781642794281 paperback
ISBN 9781642794298 eBook
Library of Congress Control Number: 2019930351

Cover and Interior Design by:
Chris Treccani
www.3dogcreative.net

Icon Designs by:
Samira Selod
www.samiraseloddesign.com

Editing by:
Andrea Jasmin
www.acjasminproofreading.com

Morgan James is a proud partner of Habitat for Humanity Peninsula and Greater Williamsburg. Partners in building since 2006.

Get involved today! Visit
MorganJamesPublishing.com/giving-back

For those who have died from opioids and their loved ones; for those who are struggling with opioid addiction and their loved ones; and for those who are working to change the trajectory of the opioid epidemic. May we all have the courage to change the things we can.

GLOSSARY

Abuse. misuse of a drug to feel euphoria; using something for a bad purpose

Addiction. the condition of continued drug use or activity despite negative consequences

Dependence. the body is reliant on drugs; the body experiences withdrawal symptoms when not taking the drug

Epidemic. an outbreak of a disease that spreads quickly and affects many individuals at one time

Euphoria. a feeling or state of intense excitement or extreme good feelings

Legitimate. conforms to the rules or laws

Misuse. taking a prescription is a way that is not intended by a doctor; using something in the wrong way

Opioid. chemical that binds to the body's opioid receptors and reduces pain

Potent. having great power, influence, or effect; strong

Prohibit. to formally forbid something by rule, law or other authority

Reinforce. strengthen or support; encourage

Relapse. return to using drugs after a period of improvement

Synthetic. made by humans

Vulnerable. susceptible to something negative; more likely

Withdrawal. the process of ceasing to take an addictive drug

Words Commonly Used by Oxen

OXams. tests and exams that an ox takes in school

OXed. past tense of ask

OXtra. when an ox has too many or extra

OXtreme biking. extreme biking when done by an ox

OXcellent. excellent from an ox's point of view

Parod(ox)y. an imitation with deliberate exaggeration while using an ox for humorous effect

IF YOU GIVE AN OX AN OXY, HE'S GOING TO ASK FOR ANOTHER.

What is an oxy?

Oxy is short for the prescription **opioid** medication oxycodone.

What is an opioid?

Prescription opioids are a group of medications that are similar to the chemicals that our body makes naturally to relieve pain and also similar to the illegal drug heroin. In nature, opioids are found in the seed pod of the opium poppy plant. Opioid medications can be:

- **Natural.** made from the plant
- **Synthetic.** completely made by people
- **Semi-synthetic.** modified in a lab from the plant

Source: National Institute on Drug Abuse; National Institutes of Health; U.S. Department of Health and Human Services. Available at: https://teens.drugabuse.gov/drug-facts/prescription-pain-medications-opioids

WHEN HE TAKES THE OXY, THE LEG HE HURT WHILE OXTREME BIKING WILL FEEL BETTER.

How do opioid medications treat pain?

- Prescription opioids usually come in pill form and are given to treat severe pain—for example, pain from surgery, serious sports injuries or cancer. For most people, when opioids are taken as prescribed by a doctor for a short time, they are relatively safe and can reduce pain effectively.

- Opioids attach to specific proteins, called opioid receptors, on nerve cells in the brain, spinal cord, gut and other organs. When these drugs attach to their receptors, they block pain messages sent from the body through the spinal cord to the brain.

- Commonly used prescription opioids include: morphine, codeine, hydrocodone, oxycodone, fentanyl, methadone and tramadol.

 **In the news, you may have heard about illegal use of opioids.**

Does it surprise you that opioids can be prescribed by doctors to treat pain?

Source: National Institute on Drug Abuse; National Institutes of Health; U.S. Department of Health and Human Services. Available at: https://teens.drugabuse. gov/drug-facts/prescription-pain-medications-opioids

WHEN HE TAKES ANOTHER HE'LL REALIZE
THAT THE OXY MAKES HIM FEEL OXCELLENT
...LIKE HE JUST WON AN OX RACE!

Why do opioids make people feel excellent?

Opioid receptors are located in the brain's reward center. When an opioid attaches to one of these receptors, it causes a large release of the chemical dopamine [**doh**-puh-meen]. Dopamine makes the body have a strong feeling of relaxation and **euphoria**, or extreme good feelings.

Laughing releases dopamine.

What other things do you think might cause the body to relax and feel good by releasing dopamine?

Source: National Institute on Drug Abuse; National Institutes of Health; U.S. Department of Health and Human Services. Available at: https://teens.drugabuse. gov/drug-facts/prescription-pain-medications-opioids

HE'LL FEEL SO OXCELLENT THAT HE'LL START TAKING MORE AND MORE OXY.

Taking a prescription opioid in a way that is not intended by a doctor is called **misuse**. According to a national survey, about 4% of 15-year-olds reported misusing opioids.

Source: Substance Abuse and Mental Health Services Administration. (2018). Results from the 2017 National Survey on Drug Use and Health: Detailed Tables. Available at: https://www.samhsa.gov/data/sites/default/files/cbhsq-reports/ NSDUHDetailedTabs2017/NSDUHDetailedTabs2017.htm#tab1-27B

What are examples of prescription opioid misuse?

1 Taking someone else's prescription, even if it is for a **legitimate** medical purpose like relieving pain.

2 Taking an opioid medication in a way other than prescribed– for example, taking more than the prescribed dose or taking it more often.

3 Taking an opioid prescription to feel euphoric, also referred to as getting high. Misusing a drug to get high is called **abuse**.

4 Mixing opioid medications with alcohol or other drugs.

Prescription medications are some of the most commonly misused drugs by teens, after tobacco, alcohol, and marijuana [mar-uh-**wah**-nuh], also known as pot.

Source: National Institute on Drug Abuse; National Institutes of Health; U.S. Department of Health and Human Services. Available at: https://teens.drugabuse. gov/drug-facts/prescription-pain-medications-opioids

HE KNOWS HE SHOULD STOP TAKING THEM BECAUSE HIS LEG HAS HEALED.

BUT HE CAN'T.

People take too many opioids for 5 main reasons.

1 Opioids don't typically control long-term or chronic pain. People often incorrectly believe that if they take more, the pain will go away.

2 Some people are **vulnerable**, or more likely, to use more opioids. For example, mental health disorders or a person's genetics can increase the risk of abuse. Because people often don't know they are vulnerable, even opioids prescribed by a doctor can lead to problems.

3 People who have abused other drugs, like alcohol or marijuana, are more likely to abuse opioids, even when they are prescribed by a doctor.

4 Using opioids can feel like it numbs emotional pain in people who have experienced trauma, like child abuse or the death of a loved one, or who have a mental health disorder. This feeling of numbness can **reinforce**, or encourage, taking too many opioids.

5 When people first use an opioid for abuse or recreation, or for non-medical uses, they are more likely to take too many or abuse opioids.

Source: Stumbo SP, Yarborough BJH, McCarty D, Weisner C, Green, CA. Patient-reported pathways to opioid use disorders and pain-related barriers to treatment engagement. *J Sub Abuse Treat*. 2017;73:47-54. Available at: https://www.journalofsubstanceabusetreatment.com/article/S0740-5472(16)30066-6/pdf

HE'LL TAKE SO MANY THAT HIS BODY WILL BECOME DEPENDENT ON OPIOIDS.

What is dependence?

- **Dependence** means the body experiences **withdrawal** symptoms, like throwing up and diarrhea, when not taking the drug. When the body withdrawals from opioids, it feels worse than the worst case of the flu.

- Carefully following the doctor's instructions for taking a medication can make it less likely that someone will develop dependence, because the medication is prescribed in amounts, forms and durations that are appropriate for that person.

Source: National Institute on Drug Abuse; National Institutes of Health; U.S. Department of Health and Human Services. Available at: https://teens.drugabuse.gov/drug-facts/prescription-pain-medications-opioids

HE TAKES SO MANY OXYS THAT HE RUNS OUT AND HAS TO ASK HIS DOCTOR FOR MORE. HIS DOCTOR SAYS NO.

Why won't doctors prescribe many pain pills?

- Prescription opioids are used to treat pain. However, they work best for short-term pain and generally don't work for long-term or chronic pain. Therefore, most doctors will only prescribe opioids for a few days–typically a week or less.

- It is important to know that scientists and doctors are always discovering and learning new information. For many years, doctors thought that opioids worked well for chronic pain. They also did not think that people would misuse opioids or become dependent. Therefore, doctors prescribed opioid pain medications to a lot of people.

- Now, scientists and doctors have learned that opioids do not work well for chronic or long-term pain and there are risks of taking opioid prescriptions.

- Therefore, most doctors will only prescribe opioids for a few days. In fact, there are laws in many states that **prohibit**, or prevent, patients from getting more than a week of prescription opioid medications at one time.

Since he can't get more from his doctor, he'll ask his friend Bull if he has any OXtra oxy leftover from after his shoulder surgery.

Where do young people get the prescription opioids they misuse?

When young people between 12 and 17 years old first start misusing opioids, they most commonly get them from a family member or friend.

It is fairly rare for young people to buy opioids from a drug dealer or stranger when they first start misusing. However, after a young person has been using for a while, they are more likely to buy from a drug dealer or stranger.

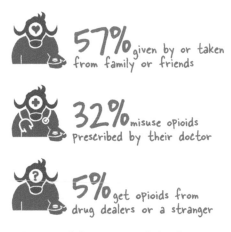

57% given by or taken from family or friends

32% misuse opioids prescribed by their doctor

5% get opioids from drug dealers or a stranger

(The remaining 6% reported the source as "other")

Source: Substance Abuse and Mental Health Services Administration. (2018). Results from the 2017 National Survey on Drug Use and Health: Detailed Tables. Available at: https://www.samhsa.gov/data/sites/default/files/cbhsq-reports/NSDUHDetailedTabs2017/NSDUHDetailedTabs2017.htm#tab6-53B

HE STARTS TAKING BULL'S OXTRA OXY. ALL HE CAN THINK ABOUT IS OXY.

HE STOPS HANGING OUT WITH HIS FRIEND BULL. HE STOPS STUDYING AND FAILS HIS OXAMS AT SCHOOL.

OX IS ADDICTED.

What is addiction?

Remember that opioids lead to the release of dopamine. Repeated surges of dopamine in the reward center of the brain from taking drugs can lead to addiction.

Addiction means that you continue to use a drug despite negative consequences.[1]

It is important to know that anyone can become addicted: rich or poor, male or female, employed or unemployed, young or old, and any race or ethnicity. Addiction is not a character defect or moral weakness, but it is a medical condition that requires professional help.[2]

 Besides not doing well in school, what other negative consequences do you think can result from drug addiction?

Sources: 1) National Institute on Drug Abuse; National Institutes of Health; U.S. Department of Health and Human Services. Available at: https://teens.drugabuse.gov/drug-facts/prescription-pain-medications-opioids

2) Center for Substance Abuse Treatment. What is substance abuse treatment? A booklet for families. HHS Publication No. (SMA) 14-4126. Rockville, MD: Substance Abuse and Mental Health Services Administration, 2004. Available at: https://store.samhsa.gov/system/files/sma14-4126.pdf

Ox is sad.

He doesn't want to be addicted.

Ox doesn't understand why he became addicted but Bull did not.

Why are some people more likely than others to become addicted?

Some people are more vulnerable than others to taking too many opioids.[1]

Here is a list of known risk factors for opioid addiction: physical pain, health problems, history of mental illness (such as anxiety and depression), abuse of other drugs, witnessing a family member overdose, or having a large number of friends who misuse prescription drugs.[1]

There is good news, however. People have a lower risk of addiction if they commit to doing well in or finishing school, have concern about the dangers of prescription drug abuse, have a strong bond with their parents, or have parents who disapprove of illegal drug use.[1]

 Youth who have used marijuana or pot are 2½ times more likely to become addicted to prescription opioids.[2]

Source: 1) Preventing prescription Drug Misuse: Understanding who is at risk. Updated May 2016. Available at: https://www.samhsa.gov/capt/sites/default/files/resources/preventing-prescription-drug-misuse-understanding.pdf; 2) Fiellin LE, Tetrault JM, Becker WC, Fiellin DA, Hoff RA. Previous use of alcohol, cigarettes, and marijuana and subsequent abuse of prescription opioids in young adults. *J Adolesc Health*. 2013;52(2):158-62. Available at: https://www.jahonline.org/article/S1054-139X(12)00231-5/pdf

WHEN HE RUNS OUT OF BULL'S OXTRA OXY, HE WILL BUY OXY FROM A STRANGER.

HE WILL TAKE TOO MANY.

HE WILL GET VERY SICK AND OVERDOSE.

What are the signs of an opioid overdose?

Signs of a possible prescription opioid overdose are:

- Slow breathing
- Blue lips and fingernails
- Cold, damp skin
- Shaking
- Vomiting or gurgling/snoring noise
- Difficult to arouse

People who are showing symptoms of overdose need urgent medical help (call 911 immediately).

Can you die of an opioid overdose?

Yes, you can overdose and die from taking too many opioids—even just once. Opioids cause the body to breathe slower. With too high of a dose, the body may stop breathing altogether.

Source: National Institute on Drug Abuse; National Institutes of Health; U.S. Department of Health and Human Services. Available at: https://teens.drugabuse. gov/drug-facts/prescription-pain-medications-opioids

669 young people under the age of 19 died of an opioid overdose in one year.

Source: Gaither JR, Shabanova V, Leventhal JM. US national trends in pediatric deaths from prescription and illicit opioids, 1999-2016. *JAMA Netw Open*. 2018;1(8):e186558. Available at: https://jamanetwork.com/journals/jamanetworkopen/fullarticle/2719580

How do people die of an opioid overdose?

- Opioids attach to receptors on nerve cells in the brain, spinal cord, gut and other organs. When these drugs attach to their receptors, not only do they block pain messages to the brain, they also slow or stop essential functions like breathing.

- The risk of overdose and death increase when opioids are combined with alcohol or other medications that also slow breathing, such as benzodiazepines (sometimes called benzos) or muscle relaxers (for example, carisoprodol or cyclobenzaprine).

- Some opioids are more **potent** than others, meaning that it takes a lower dose to create the same effect. For example, fentanyl is 50 to 100 times more potent than morphine.

- Drug dealers often make their own opioid drugs that are sold illegally on the street. These are much more deadly because they are usually made with the most potent opioids (like fentanyl) and because it is impossible to know what is actually in the drug. Opioids sold illegally on the street can be so potent that people can die from just taking one.

BULL WILL FIND HIM LYING ON THE FLOOR AND CALL AN AMBULANCE.

THE PARAMEDICS WILL SAVE HIM.

THEY WILL TAKE HIM TO THE HOSPITAL.

How can someone who has overdosed be saved from dying?

If given in time, there is a drug called naloxone [**nal**-uh k-sohn] that can reverse the effects of an opioid overdose and prevent death. Naloxone does not cure addiction. It only stops the immediate effects of opioid overdose on breathing.

Most ambulances, police officers and firefighters carry naloxone.

In many states, doctors can now prescribe naloxone in advance to people who take opioids or their family members. It can be given right away in the event of an accidental overdose, without having to wait for emergency personnel, who may not arrive in time.

In most states, pharmacists can provide naloxone to people who use prescription opioids or to their family members without the patient going to the doctor first.

 **Remember, opioids sold illegally on the street can be so potent that not even naloxone can help prevent death.**

Source: National Institute on Drug Abuse; National Institutes of Health; U.S. Department of Health and Human Services. Available at: https://teens.drugabuse. gov/drug-facts/prescription-pain-medications-opioids

WHEN HE LEAVES THE HOSPITAL, HE WILL GET TREATMENT FOR HIS OPIOID ADDICTION.

Because opioid addiction is a medical condition, it requires professional help. Opioid addiction is complex and different for each person, so there are a variety of treatment approaches.

How is opioid addiction treated?

A counselor or case manager first assesses the patient and then works with the person (and possibly their family) to develop a treatment plan. This plan lists problems, treatment goals and ways to meet those goals. Often the treatment plan includes working with a team of professionals, which may include social workers, counselors, doctors, nurses, psychologists, psychiatrists or other professionals.

Group counseling is a common part of addiction treatment. Group members usually support and try to help one another adjust to life without using drugs. They share their experiences, talk about their feelings and problems, and find out that others have similar problems. Groups also may explore faith and religion as a part of the recovery process.

 Why do you think group counseling is such an important part of treatment?

Source: Center for Substance Abuse Treatment. What is substance abuse treatment? A booklet for families. HHS Publication No. (SMA) 14-4126. Rockville, MD: Substance Abuse and Mental Health Services Administration, 2004. Available at: https://store. samhsa.gov/system/files/sma14-4126.pdf

Ox WILL START DOING BEHAVIORAL THERAPY.

What is behavioral therapy?

Behavioral therapy helps people in drug addiction treatment modify their attitudes and behaviors related to drug use. There are several types of behavioral therapy:

- **Cognitive-behavioral therapy** helps patients recognize, avoid, and cope with the situations in which they're most likely to use drugs.

- **Contingency management** provides rewards or privileges for remaining drug-free and following a treatment plan.

- **Motivational enhancement therapy** uses strategies to make the most of people's readiness to change their behavior and enter treatment.

- **Family therapy** helps people (especially young people) and their families with drug use problems, addresses influences on drug use patterns and improves overall family functioning.

- **12-step facilitation** is an individual therapy to prepare people to participate in 12-step group support programs like Alcoholics Anonymous or Narcotics Anonymous. 12-step support programs follow the themes of acceptance, surrender and active involvement in recovery.

Source: National Institute on Drug Abuse; National Institutes of Health; U.S. Department of Health and Human Services. Drugs, brains, and behavior: The science of addiction. Available at: https://d14rmgtrwzf5a.cloudfront.net/sites/default/files/soa.pdf

His doctor will treat him with medicine for his addiction.

Ox will get better.

Is there a medicine that cures addiction?

No "magic pill" exists to cure addiction, but medicines can be an important part of treatment. Medications are used for withdrawal, to reduce cravings, or to treat mental health disorders like anxiety or depression.

1 **Withdrawal:** When a person who has been taking high doses of opioids first stops, their body will go into withdrawal. There are medications that can help lessen the unpleasant symptoms of withdrawal, such as clonidine [**klon**-i-deen] and lofexidine [loe-**fex**-i-deen].

2 **Reduce cravings:** In some more severe cases, doctors will prescribe a medication as a part of a treatment program to reduce the cravings to take opioids. This is called medication-assisted therapy and is the most effective treatment for addiction. The most commonly used drugs to reduce opioid cravings are buprenorphine [**byoo**-prə-nor-fen], methadone [**meth**-uh-dohn] and naltrexone [nal-**trek**-sohn].

3 **Mental health disorders:** There is overlap between addiction and mental health disorders. In fact, half of people who are addicted will have a mental illness. The reverse is also true: half of people with a mental health disorder will become addicted. The most common mental illnesses are depression and anxiety. There are lots of medications that can treat these illnesses. Treating these conditions can make it easier to recover from addiction.

Source: Center for Substance Abuse Treatment. What is substance abuse treatment? A booklet for families. HHS Publication No. (SMA) 14-4126. Rockville, MD: Substance Abuse and Mental Health Services Administration, 2004. Available at: https://store. samhsa.gov/system/files/sma14-4126.pdf

AFTER A WHILE HE WILL START THINKING ABOUT OXY AGAIN.

Why would someone who just finished treatment start using opioids again?

About half the people who complete treatment for the first time recover. Of course, this means that about half will return to using drugs, called **relapse**, before they finally give them up for good. Adolescents are even more likely than adults to use drugs again.

Opioid addiction is often a cycle of addiction and recovery. It is not uncommon for a person to need to go through treatment more than one time. Often the person needs to return to treatment quickly to prevent a slip or relapse from leading to a chronic problem.

It is important to understand that relapse is often a part of the recovery process.

Source: Center for Substance Abuse Treatment. What is substance abuse treatment? A booklet for families. HHS Publication No. (SMA) 14-4126. Rockville, MD: Substance Abuse and Mental Health Services Administration, 2004. Available at: https://store. samhsa.gov/system/files/sma14-4126.pdf

HE WILL ASK FOR AN OXY.

And chances are if he asks for an oxy...he's going to want another one to go with it.

38

What is the best way to avoid the cycle of opioid addiction and prevent overdose death?

 Ask your doctor not to prescribe you an opioid prescription medication.

 Never misuse an opioid medication.

 Never take a drug from the street.

OXAM QUESTIONS

(answers at the bottom of page 43)

1. For most people, when opioids are taken as prescribed by a doctor for a short time, they are relatively safe.
   a. true
   b. false

2. What chemical is released into the body when opioids attach to receptors in the brain?
   a. dopamine
   b. heroin
   c. poppy
   d. euphoria

3. Taking a prescription in a way that is not intended by a doctor is called _____.
   a. abuse
   b. addiction
   c. dependence
   d. misuse

4. Misusing a drug to feel euphoric, or high, is called
   _____.
   a. abuse
   b. addiction
   c. dependence
   d. withdrawal

5. Which is **not** an example of opioid misuse?
   a. taking a friend's medicine
   b. taking your medicine how your doctor told you to
   c. mixing opioids with alcohol
   d. taking more medicine than your doctor told you to

6. Most young people who misuse opioids buy them from drug dealers or strangers.
   a. true
   b. false

7. Addiction means _____.
   a. the body experiences withdrawal symptoms when not taking the drug
   b. you continue to use a drug despite negative consequences
   c. some people are more vulnerable than others to taking too many opioids
   d. the body may stop breathing altogether

8. Addiction is a character flaw and a moral weakness.
   a. true
   b. false

9. Addiction is a medical condition that requires professional help.
   a. true
   b. false

10. Which is not a known risk factor for opioid abuse?
    a. history of anxiety
    b. abuse of other drugs
    c. having parents who disapprove of illegal drug use
    d. having witnessed someone overdose

11. You can die from taking too many opioids at one time.
    a. true
    b. false

12. What are signs of an opioid overdose?
    a. slow breathing
    b. blue lips and fingernails
    c. cold, damp skin
    d. all of the above

13. Which medication is used to reverse overdose?
    a. buprenorphine
    b. clonidine
    c. naloxone
    d. none of the above

14. Which medication is used to cure addiction?
    a. buprenorphine
    b. clonidine
    c. naloxone
    d. none of the above

15. When people complete treatment for opioid addiction, they typically never use opioids again.
    a. true
    b. false

16. What are the three best ways to avoid the cycle of opioid addiction and prevent overdose death?

Ask _____

Never_____

Never_____

FREQUENTLY OXED QUESTIONS

What is the opioid epidemic?

The opioid epidemic is a phrase used to describe the many problems caused by and related to opioid misuse and abuse. But what is an epidemic?

The dictionary defines epidemic as an outbreak of a disease that spreads quickly and affects many individuals at one time. In the study of health, the term epidemic is more specifically defined as a disease that affects more people than expected. Because most diseases don't have cures, we always *expect* that some people will have a disease. However, when more people have the disease than expected, that disease is considered an epidemic.

not an epidemic
(or expected # of
people with disease)

epidemic
(or more than expected #
of people with disease)

Today, more people are misusing, abusing, addicted to, and dying from opioids than we would expect. Addiction is a disease. That's why the phrase opioid epidemic has become a common way to describe the many problems related to opioids.

Oxy is short for oxycodone, which is sold as a prescription drug under the name OxyContin®. What are other slang or street names of pain medications?

To avoid getting in trouble, people often use slang or street names to talk about drugs in secret.

It is important that adults know about these slang terms since teenagers may use them to disguise what they are talking about. It is also important for teenagers to know about these terms so they can avoid situations where people are abusing drugs. However, slang names are always changing as people try to hide their drug abuse from others.

Common slang names of prescription pain medications include:

- **Codeine:** cody, lean, purple drank, schoolboy, syrup
- **Fentanyl:** China girl, China town, tango and cash, king ivory, murder eight, friends, goodfellas, great bear, dance fever, Apache, He-Man, jackpot
- **Hydrocodone:** (sold as a prescription medication in combination with acetaminophen called Vicodin®) hydros, lorries, tabs, vikes, vikos, Watsons, 357s
- **Oxycodone:** ox, oxy, OC, blues, hillbilly heroin, 40s, 80s (refers to the number of milligrams in each tablet)

Common slang names of the illegal drug heroin include: black tar, brown sugar, China white, dope, horse, and golden girls.

Why are there so many different names of prescription opioids, like morphine, codeine, and oxycodone?

Prescription opioids are a group made up of several medications. Medications are chemicals, and all opioid medications are chemicals that attach to opioid receptors in the human body.

Imagine that there is a lock that has multiple keys that will unlock it. The lock is the opioid receptor in the human body, and each key is an opioid medication. Some keys open the lock quickly and smoothly. Others are hard to fit into the lock and have to be twisted and turned to get the lock to open.

Each key is slightly different and opens the lock in a slightly different way.

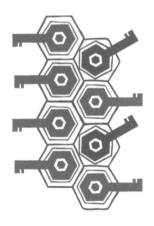

Similarly, each medication attaches to the opioid receptor slightly differently; and thus, works differently in the human body. For example, morphine works well to relieve pain, but it also makes people feel extremely tired.

Morphine is most commonly used in the hospital when someone is having surgery and needs to feel no pain. The codeine key is shaped a little different than the morphine key. It doesn't make people feel as tired, but it also doesn't relieve pain as well. Interestingly, codeine can be used to relieve pain, but it is also used in combination with other medications to reduce coughing.

Why can't people stop taking opioids?

Remember that opioids cause the release of dopamine. Dopamine is the natural chemical in the body that allows people to feel happiness. When people become addicted to drugs like opioids, the drugs become the quickest and best way for them to achieve those good feelings of happiness. In fact, the good feelings related to the drugs can be so strong that normal things that are typically enjoyable no longer give the person pleasure.

Can you imagine not feeling warm inside after a hug from someone you love? Or not feeling satisfaction after eating your favorite type of chocolate cake? A person who is addicted to opioids can only get those strong feelings of pleasure from opioids, and it takes a long time for their brains to recognize pleasure from normal sources of happiness once again after they stop taking the drug.

If prescription opioid medications are so dangerous, is it ever safe to take them?

Yes. Prescription opioid medications are a very important part of treatment for some diseases. For example, cancer is a very painful disease. When cancerous tumors grow, they can invade tissues nearby and cause pain in those areas. Many people living with cancer take prescription opioid medications regularly as an important part of their treatment.

Opioids, typically morphine or fentanyl, are used frequently in the hospital during and after surgeries to relieve pain. However, opioids are not the only medications that can be used in the hospital to relieve pain. Expert doctor groups recommend using a combination of opioid and non-opioid medications to minimize pain after surgery. This is called multimodal pain treatment. Examples of non-opioid pain medications include ibuprofen and acetaminophen.

When the patient is discharged, or sent home from the hospital, the doctor often switches the patient to combination medication that includes both an opioid and a non-opioid like ibuprofen or acetaminophen in a single pill.

After leaving the hospital, people typically do not need to take pain medications for more than a few days.

Opioids can be taken safely when taken exactly as prescribed by a doctor. However, like all medications, opioids do have risks. Patients should always discuss the risks and benefits of an opioid medication with their doctor before starting a prescription.

What should people do with leftover opioid medications?

Opioid medications, alone or in combination with other medications, are often prescribed by doctors to relieve pain after surgeries, like shoulder or knee surgeries following an injury. Doctors will typically tell patients to take the opioid pain medications until they do not need them any more to control the pain. If the doctor prescribes 7 days of medication, but the patient only needs 3 days, the patient will have 4 days of leftover opioid medications. It is important to dispose of these leftover medications, but how?

There are a few options, but the goal of all options is prevent people who were not prescribed the medications from taking them.

In the United States, the Drug Enforcement Agency has "Drug Takeback" programs every year in the fall and spring. During this time, many pharmacies, police stations, and other community organizations will take leftover medications and dispose of them properly.

If there is not a drug takeback program in your community, the next best option is to dispose of the leftover medication in the trash, following these simple rules:

1.   Remove the medication from the original prescription bottle.
2.   Mix the medication with something like dirt, slime, or kitty litter.
3.   Seal the mixture in a plastic bag.
4.   Throw the sealed container in the household trash.

There are also products available for purchase at retails stores and pharmacies that can be used to dispose of prescription medications. These products are special chemicals that, when mixed with water and medications, deactivate the drugs. After the materials are mixed, they can safely be thrown away in the trash.

What is the difference between heroin and prescription opioid medications?

Heroin is a chemical that attaches to opioid receptors in the human body. Heroin is semi-synthetic, meaning it is derived from morphine, which occurs naturally in the opioid poppy plant.

Heroin is 3 times stronger, or more potent, than the typical prescription opioid medication. That means it only takes a tiny amount of heroin to stop pain. This is very dangerous because it is very easy to take too much heroin. When a person takes too much heroin, it slows down breathing and can lead to death.

Because heroin is so dangerous, the United States government decided that it is not safe to be sold as a prescription medication. Therefore, heroin is an illegal drug.

morphine   heroin

Because heroin is chemically similar to prescription opioid medications and may be cheaper to get from drug dealers, people who have become addicted to prescription pain medications sometimes switch to using heroin. In fact, 80% percent of people who abuse heroin first misused prescription opioids. However, the transition to heroin use from prescription opioids is still rare; only about 4% of people who misuse prescription opioids use heroin. Even so, because millions of people are using prescription opioids, this adds up to hundreds of thousands of heroin users.

Source: Muhuri PK, Gfroerer JC, Davies MC. Associations of nonmedical pain reliever use and initiation of heroin use in the United States. CBHSQ Data Rev. August 2013. Available at: https://www.samhsa.gov/data/sites/default/files/DR006/DR006/nonmedical-pain-reliever-use-2013.htm

Since opioids come from the poppy plant, do poppy seeds have the same effect as opioid medications?

No. Poppy seeds found in food like breads and salad dressings do not relieve pain or produce feelings of euphoria. The parts of the poppy plant that relieve pain and produce feelings of euphoria are removed from the poppy seeds that are used in food products.

Are today's youth using as many opioids as in the past?

Without asking every single person, it is impossible to know exactly how many people are using, misusing or abusing any drug. Instead, experts use large surveys to make an estimate, or an educated guess. Researchers from the University of Michigan have been surveying people about drug use since 1975. Since they conduct the survey every year, they are able to track whether drug use is increasing, decreasing or staying the same.

In 2017, the researchers surveyed 43,000 students in 8th, 10th and 12th grades from 360 schools across the United States. What did they learn?

- Oxycodone use decreased.
- Vicodin, another common prescription opioid pain medication, use decreased.
- Heroin use decreased.

This is good news.

Source: Johnston LD, Miech RA, O'Malley PM, Bachman JG, Schulenberg JE, Patrick ME. (2018). Monitoring the Future national survey results on drug use: 1975-2017: Overview, key findings on adolescent drug use. Ann Arbor: Institute for Social Research, The University of Michigan. Available at: http://www.monitoringthefuture.org/pubs/monographs/mtf-overview2017.pdf

Do today's youth know how dangerous heroin can be—even just using it once?

The same researchers from the University of Michigan asked students how harmful they think using heroin can be. Here is what they found:

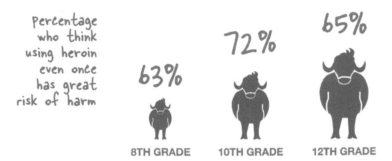

Percentage who think using heroin even once has great risk of harm

63% **8TH GRADE**

72% **10TH GRADE**

65% **12TH GRADE**

What do these percentages mean? First, they show that that 10th graders are the smartest because 72% of them know that heroin is harmful! However, these survey results also show that there are a lot of students who don't understand just how dangerous heroin and any drugs bought on the street can be.

Remember, opioids sold illegally on the street can be so potent that people can die from just taking one.

Source: Johnston LD, Miech RA, O'Malley PM, Bachman JG, Schulenberg JE, Patrick ME. (2018). Monitoring the Future national survey results on drug use: 1975-2017: Overview, key findings on adolescent drug use. Ann Arbor: Institute for Social Research, The University of Michigan. Available at: http://www.monitoringthefuture.org/pubs/monographs/mtf-overview2017.pdf

What can I do if my friends offer me drugs?

In the 1980s, young people were taught to "Just Say No" to drugs. It sounds simple, right? Sometimes it can be that simple, especially when people know just how dangerous opioids can be. However, it can also be hard to say no to your friends, especially when they pressure you. Here are two great tips so you can be prepared if you are ever faced with this situation.

1   Arrange a secret safe word with your parents or a trusted adult. When you text them this word, they will come pick you up wherever you are—no questions asked. Remember, your parents would always rather have you safe than not. A safe word can be anything, like pizza or snowflake.

2   Plan an exit strategy ahead of time and practice it. For example, "I just remembered that my mom needed me to pick up her dry cleaning before the store closes. She'll be so mad if I don't. I'll catch up with you later." It's okay to lie to get yourself out of a dangerous situation.

Remember, people who pressure you to use drugs are not your friends. Now that you know how dangerous opioids are, it's your job to teach your friends how they can stay safe.

If you or a friend are in crisis and need to speak with someone now:

Call the National Suicide Prevention Lifeline at 1-800-273-TALK
(they don't just talk about suicide–they cover a lot of issues and will help put you in touch with someone close by)

If you need information on drug treatment and where you can find it, the Substance Abuse and Mental Health Services Administration can help.

Call the Substance Abuse Treatment Facility Locator at 1-800-662-HELP

Visit the locator online at: www.findtreatment.samhsa.gov

ABOUT THE AUTHOR

Dr. Laura E. Happe, PharmD, MPH is a pharmacist, researcher and educator who uses data to help people make better decisions. As an executive leader in the pharmacy and insurance industries, Laura has developed new businesses and strategies, including the opioid epidemic response at a Fortune 50 health care company. Laura is chief editor of the peer-reviewed Journal of Managed Care and Specialty Pharmacy and a university professor of population health and managed care. She lives with her husband in Charlotte, North Carolina, where they teach their kids that happiness is a choice.

Learn more about Laura at www.laurahappe.com or contact her at lehappe@gmail.com

ABOUT THE ILLUSTRATOR

Bryan Nigh is a graphic designer, illustrator, and creator of the animated short series *Brad the Jerk Dog*. After earning a bachelor's degree in 2-D animation from Columbia College Chicago, he worked in the entertainment industry for 10 years in Los Angeles and Atlanta. As an associate producer with Bento Box Animation Studios, he contributed to several series such as *Allen Gregory*, *Brickleberry*, and *The Awesomes*. Bryan now lives in Kansas City, Missouri, with his wife and two dogs.

Learn more about Bryan Nigh's work at www.bryannigh.carbonmade.com or contact him at bryannigh@gmail.com

Printed in the USA
CPSIA information can be obtained
at www.ICGtesting.com
JSHW07195615 0824
68134JS00064B/3853

9 781642 794281